The Poetry Bridge

Elwood Buckwalter

A publication of

Eber & Wein Publishing

Pennsylvania

The Poetry Bridge

Copyright © 2014 by Elwood Buckwalter

Library of Congress
Cataloging in Publication Data

ISBN 978-1-60880-330-9

Proudly manufactured in the United States of America by

Eber & Wein Publishing

Pennsylvania

I would like to dedicate this, my first book, to my wife Hazel for her commitment to me throughout the time it took to develop it. I could not have done it without her. Also to the many friends who kept encouraging me to write this book.

So here it is; sit back and enjoy.

Today, if you will hear His voice,
do not harden your hearts.

—Hebrews 3:7

Today

Where we are now is called today.
It promises neither joy nor sorrow.
To get here, we came through yesterday,
And we are going to leave through tomorrow.

The coming and leaving is of little account
If we don't make the most of today.
Whether sorrow or joy, God works that out
When we walk in His loving way.

So be faithful in the place He has given
For you to serve Him while it is today.
Then tomorrow arriving in Heaven,
We'll forget all the struggles of yesterday.

Artist Note
Viewing the Eternal Bridge

As I sat down to write this poem, which was New Year's morning 2007, the facts and the words tumbled through my mind so fast I could hardly write them fast enough. When I completed the writing, I was amazed at what was there. It is said when a poet writes he expresses things more truthfully than anyone else. I cannot vouch for everyone, but most often when I write, I sense the direction of the almighty God Himself, and the words are His words, not mine. I can vouch that my best writings happen when I am inspired by someone much higher than myself. Believe me, just contemplate these lines from "In the Beginning," and you may find just as I did that the more I meditate on the words, the more I realize the lack of my understanding.

In the beginning God ...

—Genesis 1:1

In the Beginning

In the true sense of the word, this is a God term, *in the beginning*,
Who else but God could ever claim this position in history?
Think of it, God is the one who began history, *in the beginning*,
And all that has passed since the beginning is part of *His story*.

As we celebrate the first day of a new year, another beginning,
Let us mark this day and take time to ponder our part in history.
In this we can adjust our lives to God's plan for a new beginning,
And as we follow His plan our lives become part of *His story*.

God, in creation, made man a creature of choice, in our beginning,
Giving us the ability to determine the shape of our part in history.
The birth of God's son into the world completed man's beginning.
By accepting this as our second birth we become part of *His Story*.

Allowing Him to be Lord of our lives brings us a new beginning.
Enjoy His love, return His love—you may alter the course of history.
It's worth the risk, if there is such a thing, for He is Lord of beginning,
So indulge yourself today in His love, experiencing all of *His story*.

Now a mist went up from the earth and watered the whole face of the ground ... and made every tree to grow that is pleasant to the eye and good for food.

—Genesis 2:6 & 9

Love in Full Bloom

Not a morning person? "That's unthinkable!" I thought,
Watching this enchanting new day evolve before my eyes.
The garden of shadows danced into place as the sun taught,
Enhancing the beauty by painting its backdrop in the skies.

The mist arose quietly as the sun lifted the blanket of dew.
Meticulously this mist polishes every branch, blade and leaf
With vibrant colors in a rich luster dancing to a rainbow hew,
Embracing a serenade of beauty with an ever-changing relief.

The evolving of this scene now takes on another dimension,
With beauty completely enveloping my heart and my soul.
Birds are now chiming in with this morning convention,
Transfixed I now find my emotions totally out of control.

Now with my heart shouting praises as my lips follow suit,
I see the smile of my Creator as my feet dance to His tune.
Oh the glory of the moment even though I'm so minute,
My Lord has chosen to bless me with His love in full bloom.

God's Hourglass

Patiently waiting for God's very best in your life
May seem as if the sands of time have blown away.
Just then God picks up the hourglass of your life;
He lovingly assures you that everything is okay.

Then you settle back as the sands trickle through
In a beauty of movement you've never seen before.
Suddenly God's arms of holiness envelops you
As contentment fills your heart right where you are.

You watch God lovingly pick up your hourglass,
Moving it to a place He had chosen from the start.
Then He places it next to His own hourglass
And lovingly draws them both close to His heart.

In wonder you watch seeing God's plan unfold.
Just remember God's hourglass is always on time.
As you watch the hourglass, which you now hold,
Be assured God is watching from the other side.

Why are you cast down, O my soul?
And why are you disquieted within me?
Hope in God;
for I shall yet praise Him,
the help of my countenance and my God.

—Psalms 42:11

Artist Note
The Bridge of Waiting

My life is no different than anyone else's in the fact that
it is full of disappointments, delays and setbacks. I wrote
this poem for a close friend who had waited many long
years for mister right to come along. Finally, one day he
showed up and the fit was perfect, and it shows all the
possibilities of giving her life a story-book ending. We
all have bridges of waiting in our lives. I trust as you
read this poem it will do for you what it did for me as
you become more aware of God's plan for your life.

ENTER HERE GOD'S GARDEN OF PRAYER

The Gate Stands Ajar

Gesturing, He motions me toward the garden gate.
Overwhelmed, I see Him holding the gate ajar.
Drawn by a sliver of beauty just waiting to escape,
Silently I stand wondering, have I already gone too far?

Gasping, I sense a fresh rush of turmoil and peace,
As He smiles and slowly swings the gate open wide.
Riveting my gaze on His holy eyes, I'm lost for speech,
Dropping to my knees, helplessly humbled by His side.
Engulfed by His presence, is it a trance or a dream?
Nothing else matters now as time seems to stand still.

Overflowing love washes through my entire being,
Faith and grace now melting together into His will.

Preparing me for a new wholeness I would experience,
Radiance of His love surrounds me like the purest gold,
Auroras of His beauty confirming His holy existence,
Yielding my will completely, allowing His to unfold.
Every day now I find rest here in His garden of prayer,
Restoring my soul to carry His love to a cold, dark world.

Then those who went before and those followed cried out saying,
"Hosanna! Blessed is he who comes in the name of the Lord!
Blessed is the kingdom of our father David
that comes in the name of the Lord!
Hosanna in the highest."

—Mark 11:9–10

Palm Sunday

A light mist was rising from the valley below,
The night shadows slipping away from the sun.
I stepped outside to inhale this beautiful flow;
Of the birth of Sabbath, which had just begun.

Down the valley road I spied a joyous parade,
The sounds were those of people praising God
With palm branches waving in a great serenade
As they removed their coats for covering the sod.

As I pondered this scene there was Jesus my Lord
In the midst on a donkey as the crowd began to sing.
Excited they chimed, "Glory to God!" in one accord,
"All power to Him who now comes as our King."

As this engulfing procession passed by my home,
I just had to participate; there was no other way.
So I joined in praising God with a branch of my own,
Blessed to be part of what's called Palm Sunday.

A Good Friday?

With the lushest aroma of spring's first flowers,
The enchanting concert of the beckoning birds
Sets a beautiful scene of enjoyment for hours,
Which allows your heart to just fill in the words.

This tranquil beauty was lost in a sudden blast;
I heard shouts of an approaching angry hoard.
"What could incite any frenzy like this?" I gasped,
"Oh no! It can't be! They are beating my Lord!"

Suddenly my whole being seemed to come apart,
For all I now lived for was wrapped up in Him.
What could I do? Such love for Him filled my heart.
That could not change, for He had forgiven my sin.

My hopes now dashed, I stood frozen to the spot,
Not wanting to watch but I couldn't run away.
Only days before I had witnessed that joyous plot,
And I had hoped this would be a good Friday.

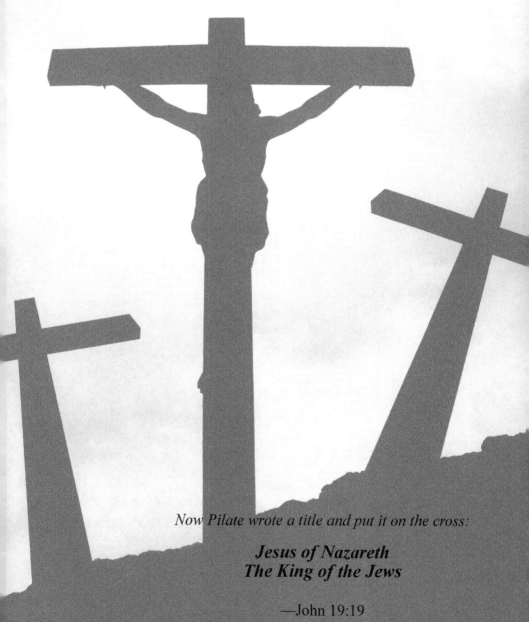

Therefore when the chief priests and officers saw Him, they cried out, saying, "Crucify Him, crucify Him." Pilate said to them, "You take Him and crucify Him, for I find no fault in Him."

—John 19:6

Now Pilate wrote a title and put it on the cross:

Jesus of Nazareth
The King of the Jews

—John 19:19

"But you shall receive power when the Holy Spirit has come upon you, and you shall be witnesses to me in Jerusalem and in all Judea and Samaria and to the end of the earth."

—Acts 1:8

The Christ of Easter

A chill of death gripped the air of the morning.
We numbly wondered, could we face another day?
Scenes of Friday's crowd in my mind kept replaying,
Hearing "Crucify Him, crucify Him, take Him away!"

As wearily we watched Mary burst into the room.
She exclaimed, "His body is not there, it's gone!"
Now Peter and John raced off for the garden tomb,
Bewildered when they realized Mary was not wrong.

Mechanically Mary sat totally engulfed in her grief,
When she heard "Mary," as Jesus called her by name.
Now her grieving gave way to wonder and disbelief
As slowly she absorbed the scene, *can He be the same?*

Then suddenly assurance grabbed hold of her soul
As He told her, "Go tell my disciples and Peter."
So this same assurance, not in part but the whole,
Is ours when we encounter the Christ of Easter.

When ... I Am

When I see Jesus in the full aurora of His kingly royalty,
I am made painfully aware of my wretched condition.
When I see Jesus pure in holiness with crystallizing beauty,
I am absorbed by the filthy rags of my human position.

When I see Jesus' face, He knows me through and through.
I am struck down motionless, unable to escape His gaze.
When I see Jesus loving or condemning, what will He do?
I am feeling His love, but judgment has my mind in a haze.

When I hear Jesus' voice, deep resilience calling me by name,
I am lying helpless with every fiber of my being exhausted.
When I feel Jesus' assurance, I know I will never be the same.
I am aware of His loving forgiveness now being fully entrusted.

When I hear Jesus' word penetrating every corner of my soul,
I am speechless as I stand in the pure holiness of His love.
When I see Jesus brilliant in pure holiness making me whole,
I am blessed in this brilliance, so I to others reflect His love.

Oh the freedom in His mercy,
Oh the wonder of His Love,
I am His and His completely
Until I reach my home above.

"Woe is me for I am undone!
Because I am a man of unclean lips,
and I dwell in the midst of a people of unclean lips;
for my eyes have seen the King, the Lord of hosts."

Then I said, "Here am I; send me."

—Isaiah 6:5 & 8

You shall be like a watered garden,
and like a spring of water,
whose waters do not fail.

—Isaiah 55:11

Bloom Where You Are

Flowers may grow in the most unlikely place,
Unlike people who seem to spring up everywhere.
One thing these two share regardless of the space,
It was in God's plan to have put them there.

Remember you are not where you are by mistake,
Oh no! You were put there for a very good reason.
The Master Gardener knows just who it will take
In beautifying His garden through every season.

Today you may feel lost out on the garden fringe
With no familiar backdrop, only vast open space.
But bloom on, even though you may want to cringe;
The Gardener's not finished, He knows your place.

Just go ahead and bloom with all of your strength,
Trusting the Master Gardener's plan is better by far.
For the love of His garden He will go to all length,
Helping you be His best, to bloom where you are.

Train up a child in the way he should go.
When he is old he will not depart from it.

Proverbs 22:6

Once Upon a Time

"Mommy, read me a story." My favorite book in hand,
I'd bound into the kitchen just before going to bed.
Sitting down she'd pull me close. She'd say, "Let's see if we can,"
Another continued story already rooted in my head,
Painting incredible pictures on the canvas of my mind,
Pictures yet today untarnished in my memory shrine.

Just as *once upon a time* and *lived happily ever after*
Suggest a beginning that goes on without an end,
Gradually changing *in the beginning, God our creator*,
She would reveal completely God's love without end.

Time moved on.
We all grew older somehow but never seemed to notice,
Until *once upon a time* now is only a fond memory;
Or is it? I don't think so.

Once upon a time is the stage where life is played out.
A master at mind pictures, mother would set this stage.
For the next episode of life promised to be a sell-out,
And she was not about to miss even the first page.

Without missing the cue, picking up God's brush of love,
She gracefully brushed this love to just the right blend,
Bringing rich hews of grace drawn from Heaven above,
Mother's *happily ever after* is God's love without end.

He who finds a wife finds a good thing, and finds favor from the Lord.

—Proverbs 18:22

I Still Do

It seems like only yesterday
You were dressed in white and I in blue,
When with two little words we would say,
Forever and ever, "I do."

Wedding flowers usually are white
With a touch of red or a touch of blue,
But the lasting love will only be right,
As we live the forever and ever, "I do."

Now fifty years to the day,
Our clothes may not have the same hue,
But those two little words I will always say,
Forever and ever, "I do."

I love you.
Forever and ever, "I do."

Your lips, O my spouse,
drip as the honeycomb;
honey and milk are under your tongue,
and the fragrance of your garments
are like the fragrance of Lebanon.

—Song of Solomon 4:11

Rose Petals of Love

Like roses splashed with the morning dew,
Each droplet carrying a rainbow of light,
So fragile the beauty and always brand new,
It's God's way of saying everything is all right.

When I look into your eyes and say *I love you*,
Like dewdrops our tears are a rainbow of light.
So fragile this beauty each morning is renewed,
It's God, He promised us everything is all right.

Like the rose, life is fragile, handle it with care,
Enjoying its beauty before the petals fall.
Its fragrance lingering, handle it with prayer,
It's God's love expressed as the petals fall.

Today is a most beautiful rose I give to you.
Enjoy the fragrance and beauty from above.
Tomorrow and beyond I will always love you,
Our pathway covered with rose petals of love.

Dance Like No One Is Watching

Twenty-one years ago you came dancing into our lives.
You've done it with total abandoned grace and poise.
So it is when you totally focus on God's leading eyes,
Completely undaunted by life's confusion and noise.

Having enjoyed the opportunity we've been given,
Watching your life dance improve through the years,
Giving us memories to cherish all the way to Heaven,
For the passion you've shared through hope and tears.

You just continue dancing while there's still time.
As life's dance continues, just follow the Lord's lead.
He'll give you new music with which you'll do fine
While you're adjusting to His new tempo and speed.

Remember all your friends will be cheering you on,
As your life dance continues with the greatest of ease,
Sharing with others how this dance should be done
And always knowing it's your Lord you will please.

Give unto the Lord the glory due to His name;
worship the Lord in the beauty of holiness.
For you have turned my mourning into dancing
and have clothed me with gladness.

—Psalms 29:2 & Psalms 30:11

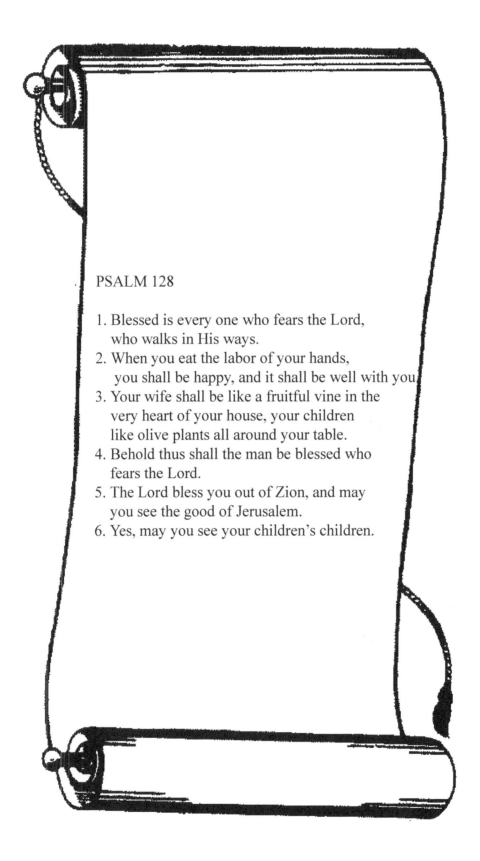

PSALM 128

1. Blessed is every one who fears the Lord,
   who walks in His ways.
2. When you eat the labor of your hands,
   you shall be happy, and it shall be well with you.
3. Your wife shall be like a fruitful vine in the
   very heart of your house, your children
   like olive plants all around your table.
4. Behold thus shall the man be blessed who
   fears the Lord.
5. The Lord bless you out of Zion, and may
   you see the good of Jerusalem.
6. Yes, may you see your children's children.

Reflections by Grandpa

Today I looked back over my life's short span.
This is only a spot on the wall of time,
But in this spot was God's eternal plan.
With His finger of love He drew my lifeline.

He drew this lifeline through my mother's love,
As I awoke to behold my first day on Earth.
Through my years she taught me of the God above,
Helping me to learn what this lifeline was worth.

Excitement of this worth, He drew the lifeline longer,
Stretching me to reach for new heights in my life.
He saw I needed some help so I could grow stronger,
So He gave me the gift of Hazel, a true, loving wife.

Now driven by wild anticipation and a lot of dreams,
We plunged forward in this new life with a passion.
In a flash, time moves this lifeline through the scenes,
When suddenly a new mother bursts out in full fashion.

Our strength developed as we grew with each other,
Exploding in full brilliance to a brand new horizon.
Hazel, my loving wife now becomes a true mother
With a beautiful gift coming from this loving union.

Standing in awe we see God draw this lifeline again,
As we would make room for this new life to come.
The joy of holding you as we felt the new life begin,
Now because of you, Susan, we are truly one.

With life rushing on at the speed of light,
We guided you in the growing up years.
We may not have always done everything right,
But you always brought us more joy than tears.

This lifeline now draws you as wife in your home
And the mother of two lovely girls of your own.
You're more the pride of our life and the life to come,
As you honorably keep these lifelines going on.

Artist Note
Viewing the Bridge of Memories

Looking back from the vantage point of sixty-plus years, I become increasingly aware of the part memories play in developing one's total life. As I wrote "Painting Memory Pictures," I realized we need both good and bad experiences to paint a life portrait. In doing so, we understand that even the worst memories are needed to complete a life passionately lived to the fullest. The constraining binds of life we all experience take on a new beauty when painted into the backdrop of your memory picture.

A man who has friends
must himself be friendly,
but there is a friend who
sticks closer than a brother.

—Proverbs 18:25

Painting Memory Pictures

As dawn's first glimmer brightens the eastern sky,
The mocking bird sings her first morning song.
Her task, wakening all nature the month of July;
The sweet notes of this routine won't take long.

Slivers of sunbeams lace through the trees,
Like weaving a basket for a picnic today.
Willow branches gracefully move in the breeze,
Beckoning me to come along and play.

Caught up in the tantalizing movement of beauty,
I just had to be part of this engulfing motion.
The old fishing pole gave me a sense of my duty,
And the sun-weathered hat confirmed my emotion.

So donning my hat and grabbing my old fishing pole,
I headed out to be part of this awesome display.
Lounging in the sweet grass by the old fishing hole
Promised only the best for this beautiful day.

My dog Shep resting dutifully right by my side
Seemed to enjoy the moments this day we'd spend.
We both agreed nothing is better than being outside,
Being painted into the picture with your best friend.

Backdrops of memory pictures like these,
Painted on the canvas walls of our minds,
Give us the exclusive rights to be at ease
When life seems to put us in constraining binds.

Just lay back in the lush love of nature's Creator,
For loving forgiveness is all that is on His mind,
Allowing Him to paint you into His great picture,
Holding you as His best friend for now and all time.

Do not forget to entertain strangers,
for by so doing, some have unwittingly
entertained angels.

—Hebrews 13:2

The Stranger

One day this stranger arrived from somewhere;
No one could ever find out from just where.
He always had this contagious smile and grin,
Making everyone he met wonder about him.
Then he was gone and no longer there.

The people wondered as they walked to and fro,
Questioning each other, doesn't anyone know?
Whenever seeing him made my day worthwhile,
Others would agree and couldn't help but smile.
For now his work was done, so he had to go.

Many years later after this stranger came to town,
Mention the nameless stranger, people turn around.
If you take notice, they will have a radiant smile.
Pondering the stranger still makes the day worthwhile;
Never uttering a word he turned this town upside down.

So my friend, take your Christ out into the street.
You need not be loud, for God will use the meek.
You may be God's angel for some lost soul today,
And if it's only a smile, you must give it away.
You may be that stranger they remember next week.

True Godly Love

True godly love is always sincere;
All evil it hates with a passion,
Clings to all good things, holding them dear,
With devoted love, shows compassion.

True godly love honors others above oneself,
Serving the Lord and others in Godly fervor,
Joyfully hopes in faithful prayer above all else,
Being patient in affliction, complaining never.

True godly love shares with those in need,
Always practicing hospitality with one another.
Then we can bless those who curse us indeed
Because of the strength we gain from each other.

True godly love rejoices with others, from the heart
And mourns with them as deep waters they go through.
When living in harmony, conceit will never have a part;
Our association will not be limited to the *who's who*.

True godly love never repays evil for evil,
Courageously living upright before everyone's eyes,
As much as possible, lives at peace with all people,
Others may look on with wonder and surprise.

True godly love never takes revenge in its own way,
Always leaving room for God's love to shine through.
God has written, "Vengeance is mine, I will repay,"
So we seek only the good for others to do.

True godly love may see his enemy hungry or thirsty
And will supply these needs with loving compassion.
You rejoice in the blessing of sharing God's mercy.
The enemy will never forget your love in this fashion.

True godly love will never be overcome by evil,
But in all things will overcome evil with good.
And oh the blessings we receive as God's people
When living out true godly love as we should.

Now abides faith, hope and love, these three;
but the greatest of these is love.

—1 Corinthians 13:13

But whosoever shall offend one of these little ones who believe in me, it were better for him that a millstone were hung about his neck, and that he were drowned in the depth of the sea.

—Matthew 18:6

Walk Ever So Softly

We touch many lives for a short period of time,
Leaving our footprints impressed on their hearts.
Walk ever so softly through each human shrine,
Leaving your footprints of love on their hearts.

It's only a few moments until we'll be parted
With these moments forever being frozen in time.
Each life we touch will move on more lighthearted.
In return our heart will take on a new rhyme.

Lord, help me with all the lives I touch today,
As I walk ever so softly and not to be rushed,
Leaving Your footprints of love all the way,
So no heart You give me will ever be crushed.

Artist Note
Love Prints Bridge All Time

I wrote this poem for Mother's Day this past year. Viewing society's understanding, or misunderstanding, of the important role a mother plays in all of our lives, I can't help feeling that we are being misled. Reflecting on my life, seeing all the mothers whose lives touched mine, I'm so thankful I had the opportunity to have grown up in a close-knit generation where mothers were mothers in the truest sense of the word. I, myself, am a person who enjoys feeling life with my heart, allowing my heart to communicate my emotions, especially in writing. This I attribute to the fact of having a mother, grandmother, mother-in-law, and a wife who all left "love prints" all over my heart.

Mothers, do not let your beauty be that outward adorning, but let it be the hidden person of the heart.

—1 Peter 3:3–4

Love Prints

Many important men who walked on this earth
Thought they were a special gift to mankind.
In many ways they tried to prove their worth,
Leaving their footprints in the sands of time.

As sands are washed by the waves of life,
The footprints of these men will disappear,
Leaving only a memory of his boastful strife;
It is soon forgotten he was ever here.

But someone else who leaves prints behind
Does not need boast, saying, "I am here."
For her presence has touched all mankind,
And the prints she leaves will not disappear.

This person placed here by God above
Brings quietness to life and makes us whole.
This can only be found in a mother's love,
Leaving her love prints on our heart and soul.

"Prove Me now in this," says the Lord of hosts,
"and see if I will not for you open the windows of heaven
for you ... and pour out such a blessing on you that there
will not be room enough to receive it."

—Malachi 3:10

A Window of Time

We all have been given a window;
We call it our window of time.
What we see as we look through this window
Gives direction to your life and mine.

As I talked this morning with my Lord,
He framed my world in this space,
Bringing my heart and His into one accord,
So all I saw now was His loving grace.

Then He opened a door we both walked through,
Showing me a world of violence and crime.
He said, "It's My grace that I give unto you;
Share it freely in your window of time.

This morning as I look through this window,
Is it your life I'll see in this space?
If it is, I'm praying for you as I continue,
So through me you'll see God's loving grace.

That's My Father

In loving memory of Lloyd Buckwalter

It seems like only yesterday
People referred to me as laddie.
When asking, "Who are you with today?"
I'd look up with joy and say, "That's my daddy."

Getting older, I learned about growing pains.
There were times when I was just plain bad.
With a little correction that could bring tear stains,
He lovingly set me straight because *that's my dad*.

In my high school years, which passed so fast,
Getting in trouble only seemed to be a bother.
They would call me the preacher's kid as they passed,
So I would just proudly say, "That's my father."

It's with great joy today, as I look back through the years,
Seeing how you taught me as we spent time with each other.
Your God is now my God through my joy and my tears,
And because of your love I can say, "He's my Father."

Thank you, Daddy,
For being my dad.
A true loving father,
Showing me God the Father.

"Well done good and faithful servant; you were faithful over a few things. I will make you ruler over many things. Enter into the joy of your Lord."

—Matthew 25:21

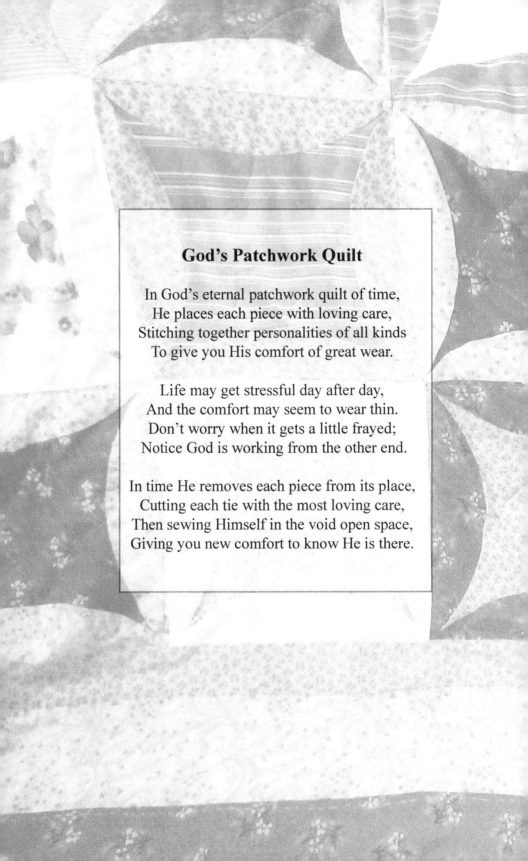

God's Patchwork Quilt

In God's eternal patchwork quilt of time,
He places each piece with loving care,
Stitching together personalities of all kinds
To give you His comfort of great wear.

Life may get stressful day after day,
And the comfort may seem to wear thin.
Don't worry when it gets a little frayed;
Notice God is working from the other end.

In time He removes each piece from its place,
Cutting each tie with the most loving care,
Then sewing Himself in the void open space,
Giving you new comfort to know He is there.

The Spirit also helps in our weakness, making intercession for us with groaning that cannot be uttered.... And we know that all things work together for good to those who love God, to those who are called according to His purpose.

—Romans 8:26 & 28

Artist Note
Crossing the Eternal Bridge

I wrote this poem in memory of my mother the day of her passing on to her eternal reward.

She lived November 23, 1919—June 7, 2012.

She lived to the fullest, gracefully stepping across the "Eternal Bridge" from time.

"Let not your heart be troubled.
In my father's house are many mansions;
I go to prepare a place for you.
And if I go to prepare a place for you,
I will come again to receive you unto myself,
that where I am there you may be also."

—John 14:1–3

Fading Sunset

As I view the beauty of an evening sunset,
I reflect on life's end of a godly mother
Who would rise early at the time God had set,
Walking daily planning for God's forever.

Life took on meaning through her youthful glow.
She was challenged to full strength at its height.
Then in the shadows of time things began to slow.
She struggled to stay, putting up a valiant fight.

But like the sunset, which only lasts a short while
With its beauty etched on the walls of our minds,
So this godly mother has passed on with a smile,
Stepping into the eternal, released from all time.

Now with the sunset's beauty in faded reserve,
The eternal day for this mother has just begun,
Peacefully resting with the one she had served,
Experiencing more beauty than any setting sun.

Mourning to Morning

With all my love and prayers
to my grieving friend

Sitting here on the north slope of life once again,
The sun over my shoulder makes the shadows long.
I realize the depth of the last farewell of a friend,
   Trying to envision the place where he's gone.

I slowly rise as the cold night envelops my soul,
Only to stop and sigh a final farewell to my friend;
For we had spent the years together with the goal
Of celebrating our lives together to the very end.

Why God chose to take you and leave me behind
My heart is broken too much now to understand.
By faith I'm trusting God's love to help me find
The strength resting under His tender loving hand.

Today, walking by faith, tears clouding my sight,
I hold to the scriptures to comfort my mourning.
I now read, weeping may last through the night,
   But it's true that joy will come in the morning.

Weeping may endure for the night.
But joy comes in the morning.

—Psalms 30:5b

Lord, who shall abide in Thy tabernacle?
Who shall dwell in Thy holy hill?
He that walks uprightly, works righteously,
and speaks the truth in his heart.

—Psalms 15:1–2

All Is Well

Standing here today in my timber shrine,
While resting, I reflect on the years;
There hanging on the walls of my mind,
A full gallery of pictures appear.

Men who may draw the gaze of a crowd
While traveling through life on this earth,
And others who are shouting out loud,
Just to prove to the world what they're worth.

Then my eyes are drawn to one picture
Of a man I had met many years ago,
His life framed in a humble demeanor,
Surrounding all who came near in its glow.

Israel Ruth, my grandfather, was the inscription,
So elegantly written out below.
He served the Lord with great satisfaction,
Showing others the right way to go.

He learned from his Lord what was good,
And all that the Lord would require.
He did justly, loving mercy, as he should,
Walking humbly before his God, inspired.

As I stood there gazing through joyful tears,
The scene seemed to change once again.
While the Lord seemed to envelop the years,
He and Israel walked off hand in hand.

Watching them for a while, I then turned to go,
Feeling a new sense of joy in my soul.
For the love of God enveloped me so,
I knew deep in my heart all is well.

Mosby's Rainbow of Love

At the end of the rainbow, so we've been told,
there's a treasure, and find it we must;
so as we went searching for our pot of gold,
it was you, Mosby, there waiting for us.

Igniting the red-hot passion of a kinship,
exploding with bright orange of pure delight,
we recall the warm yellow glow of friendship,
when we invited you to become part of our life.

Envisioning the green pastures of enchantment,
absorbed in the backdrop of the deep velvet blue,
with enriching touches of indigo enticement,
the horizons were limitless for us to subdue.

Over the years as we tread through life's field
sprinkled full with violet flowers of love,
we learned the treasure this rainbow would yield
through the commitment to our God above.

Love, like the rainbow we always admire,
is the most beautiful sight after the storm.
So is our love, of which we never tire,
for this blooms fresh for us every morn.

Now reflecting back over the past years,
we can't thank God enough for giving us you.
When the tough times would bring us to tears,
Mosby, your love would help carry us through.

This rainbow God gave us right from the start,
now once again gives us the courage to press on;
for He knew without it, we may lose heart
and never make it through to another dawn.

Mosby, our life together was more than a rainbow,
but a journey of love, right from the start.
Each day God gave us to learn to know you,
we found more room for our love in your heart.

If at the rainbow's end, a pot of gold was all we found,
this would have been a paltry sum at best.
But finding you has made our life abound.
Thank you, Mosby, for giving us your best.

Resting in peace
with my Creator

We know that all things work together for good to them that love God, to them who are called according to His purpose.

—Romans 8:28

Watching God's Plan

Waiting for God's plan in our life,
Watching the moments pass by—
Just then God steps into our life,
Assuring us that everything is okay.

The first Christmas, angles heralded
A message never heard before.
God's holiness enveloped the world
As baby Jesus arrived at our door.

Today knowing history of the past,
God arrived as planed from the start,
Changing all from the first to the last,
Lovingly binding them close to His heart.

Watching as God's plan would unfold,
We remember God is always on time.
Watching from the place we now hold,
God is watching from the other side.

My Best Friend

I first noticed Him. I was having a heavy day,
He was standing by the road near the bend.
He just smiled as I passed and went on my way.
I thought to myself, *could it be I know Him?*

Later again I saw Him, I was tired and sore,
For the load I carried nearly had me done in.
Our eyes now met as He smiled once more.
Then reaching out he asked, "May I be your friend?"

I don't know, I thought, but it would be a relief
If He could help me carry this load to the end.
Effortless He took the whole load to my disbelief,
Then lovingly asked, "Shall we go on, my friend?"

Delightfully weightless I walked on with new hope,
The path glistening as we talked getting to know Him.
Then as we reached the crest of my hard-time slope,
His compassionate eyes asked, "Am I now your friend?"

"Oh yes! Oh yes!" I said as my anxious heart asked,
"How can I ever repay You for all You have given?"
Embracing me in tender love, He gave this task,
"Just show My love to others by being their friend."

So when reading these lines with an open heart,
You'll experience the God on whom I depend.
Release your hurts to Him right from the start;
Then you'll find Jesus will be your best friend.

Artist Note

All my life I have been privileged to have and enjoy friends. I was born into a close-knit family, but also a family that would reach out beyond the family limits to be a friend to anyone. Through this atmosphere of developing friends, I became aware of the importance of making lasting friendships. Today more than ever, my life is involved in the continual development of friendships and being a friend to as many people as I meet. The friend introduced in this poem is my best friend—not only mine, but anyone who has ever met Him says He too is their best friend. So enjoy this poem written from my own experience. I trust if you have never met Him, you will someday have this life-changing experience and will say, "He is my best friend."

A man to have friends must himself be friendly.
But there is a friend who sticks closer than a brother.

—Proverbs 18:24

Let the word of God dwell in you richly in all wisdom, teaching and admonishing one another, in psalms and hymns and spiritual songs, singing with grace in your hearts unto the Lord.

—Colossians 6:16

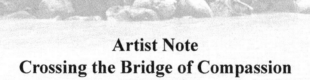

Artist Note
Crossing the Bridge of Compassion

This poem was born out of an experience where a very close friend made some bad choices, which cost him everything, and he will spend most of his life imprisoned. Experiences like this have taught me how to reach out and carry my friends to God so they can once again learn to understand His heart and experience His grace and love. Nothing is more gratifying than being chosen by God to cross the bridge of compassion and bring His love to the hurting.

Listen to God's Heart

The day was a beautiful, warm summer day,
One of those days we describe as perfect.
Everything just seemed to go the right way,
So who would dare to change this effect?

My heart rejoiced in absorbing the beauty;
I was totally unaware of an oncoming wrath.
Dark clouds were gathering in all their cruelty,
Determined to destroy everything in their path.

The news of the storm hit me most furiously,
As I heard my friend had fallen real hard.
He was bleeding and dying, I stood helplessly,
My heart screaming silently, "Oh no, God!"

Days turned to months and months to years,
Daily learning from God how to do my part.
My heart now silent, eyes glisten with tears,
God's spirit whispers, "Just listen to my heart."

My friend, I want the time to hold you close,
So together we can listen to God's heart.
Our tears will reveal the rainbow of His love,
Cleansing the pain, just listening to His heart.

Eternal Friendships

As today I think back over the years,
Remembering all the friends I've ever made
Brings a rush of joy with emotion and tears.
They were there through life's sunshine and shade.

Many friendships were born on childhood slopes,
As they developed like a slow-motion scene.
Through the growing up years exploding with hopes,
Fueled by this friendship we embarked on our dream.

Like grabbing the tale of a high-flying kite,
Life tugs on friendship nearly tearing the seam.
But it's this kind of stuff that bonds us tight,
And the most beautiful friendships would gleam.

This circle of friends enlarged with the growing years,
As we advanced through life's central plains.
Even now as I listen I can hear their cheers
Carrying me through life's losses and gains.

Now with the north slope of life drawing near,
I'm transfixed in what seems to be a dream.
Then suddenly bursting into full view you appear,
Again we're totally involved in the friendship scene.

So when you read this, I'll be thinking of you,
And just remembering you in our life makes me smile.
Even if the memories are old, they're as good as new,
For your friendship has enriched my life through each mile.

A friend loves at all times,
and a brother is born for adversity.

—Proverbs 17:17

Artist Note
Crossing the Beloved Bridge of Love

As early as I can remember, I enjoyed anything to do with reading and writing, but I was especially intrigued by poetry. Being born and raised just following the Great Depression, life was lived in a way that everything and everyone was important. I was taught from a very young age that enjoying life was a choice. As a result, I developed a very optimistic outlook on life, which I feel was the greatest motivator in my quest of reading, because the learning is endless and the experience is always worth the trip. Another thing I feel is one of the greatest assets to a writer is taking time to listen to other people, especially an older person. Poetry has become the beloved bridge through which I love to express my true feelings. I have learned even an enemy cannot hate you when you communicate in love, and there is no poem that can be written in hate because poetry does not rhyme with hate.

A Celebrated Friend

As the sun rises on each new day,
God has a great plan for you set apart;
It's something special in His loving way,
Coming straight from the Master's heart.

Life may get heavy from morning to night,
God knew this, so He created the friend.
As this friend, my heart will hold you tight,
Encouraging you to be strong to the end.

So make this a special day and celebrate
The years you've already come through.
Remember God still thinks you're great,
And He wants to celebrate with you.

I too want to celebrate with you,
For in my heart you're one great friend
Sharing together in this life as we do,
Nothing is greater than a good friend.

"One thing is needed and Mary has chosen that good part, which will not be taken away from her."

—Luke 10:41–42

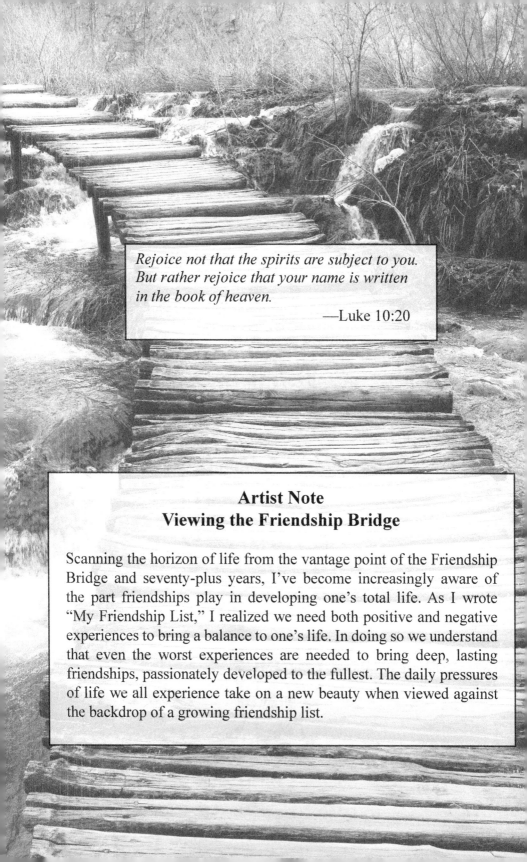

> *Rejoice not that the spirits are subject to you. But rather rejoice that your name is written in the book of heaven.*
>
> —Luke 10:20

Artist Note
Viewing the Friendship Bridge

Scanning the horizon of life from the vantage point of the Friendship Bridge and seventy-plus years, I've become increasingly aware of the part friendships play in developing one's total life. As I wrote "My Friendship List," I realized we need both positive and negative experiences to bring a balance to one's life. In doing so we understand that even the worst experiences are needed to bring deep, lasting friendships, passionately developed to the fullest. The daily pressures of life we all experience take on a new beauty when viewed against the backdrop of a growing friendship list.

My Friendship List

I have a list of friends I know, all written in a book.
So every now and then I go to take another look.
This is when again I realize these friends are just a part,
Not of the book they're written in, but they're taken from the heart.

Each name stands for someone who's crossed my path sometime;
In that meeting they've become the reason for this rhyme.
Although it sounds fantastic for me to make this claim,
I really am composed of each remembered name.

Although you're not aware of any special link,
Just know you shaped my life more than you could think.
So please don't think my greeting as just a mere routine,
Your name was not forgotten from anywhere in between.

For when I send a greeting that is addressed to you,
It is because you're on the list of friends I'm indebted to.
So whether I have known you for many days or few,
In some way you have a part in shaping things I do.

For I am but the total of the many friends I've met.
You're a friend I would prefer never to forget.

Thank you for being a true friend.

The Portrait

Standing here today, I'm enjoying the view,
With scenes of the past in everything we find.
As we sort through pictures both old and new,
One familiar face keeps showing up all the time.

With a closer look, I recognize that familiar face,
With memories and emotions coming in one blend.
Sitting back and relaxing from this searching pace,
I envision great times I've enjoyed with my friend.

Viewing the canvas of the past twenty years,
The brush strokes take on a much brighter hue.
With that brush in the hand of a God who cares,
And a man of integrity with a heart that is true.

Tom, my son, as you gave God the brush of your life,
Allowing Him to paint you in our family portrait,
Becoming our son, taking our daughter as your wife,
Has brought us great blessing we will never forfeit.

So today as we frame this portrait of time,
Stretching the canvas tight on the frame,
The beauty of this masterpiece is so sublime,
I look to see who is the signature of fame.

Awestruck when seeing the signature of God,
I'm suddenly aware His creation is not through.
We are humbled and blessed while here on this sod,
For God has privileged us to share our lives with you.

Artist Note
The Bridge of Poetry

Today, as I sit here communicating my soul with you, my mind flips back the pages of my life's photo album. I'm struck by the intense beauty of each portrait emblazoned on the canvas of time. My personal album begins just following the Great Depression in the early 1940s in central Pennsylvania. Born into a family with a deep-rooted belief in the Creator God and strong, true family ties, I learned early that with this kind of committed love to God and each other, there is only one fitting way to express the feelings of my soul, and that is through poetry. Building bridges through the art of poetry is a great way to communicate your soul to others. "The Portrait" was written for the celebration of my son-in-law's retirement from twenty years in the navy. As you read this poem, insert the name of your loved one or just someone special to you and enjoy the albums your mind unfolds.

"I am the Alpha and the Omega, the Beginning and the End, the First and the Last."

The grace of our Lord Jesus Christ be with you all. Amen.

—Revelation 22: 13 & 21

The Day of 9-11-2001

This morning dawned in bright new splendor,
While America awoke with full anticipation;
Each one going out to earn his own fair tender,
Unaware this day would forever change our nation.

But then suddenly from the sky of beautiful blue,
A terrorist violently rapes our nation's freedom;
Transfixed in the wake, not knowing what to do,
Horrified as our beloved ones die in the mayhem.

Shocked, not understanding what has been done,
While we comfort those wounded and dying,
We realize we must come back to square one,
Standing before God in truth, no more lying.

Now in truth, are we *One Nation Under God*?
If so, pledge ourselves to the Red, White and Blue,
Then rebuilding the freedom bridge back to God,
And renewing our pledge to Him while we do.

Returning our nation's God to His rightful place—
In our government, our schools and our homes—
We will raise a monument of this awful disgrace
Because we tried, without God, to do it on our own.

Then "God Bless America" we can once again sing,
With a heart full of sorrow and joy unsuppressed;
For the loss of today in our minds will always ring,
But also the joy and love for our God we confess.

Artist Note
Our Nation's Freedom Bridge

I sat down at my computer on that fateful day of the terrorist attack with my head spinning, not being able to make sense of anything, I started to write, not knowing what would come out of it. After a few minutes and a couple of lines, the thoughts tumbled through my mind and on to the page so fast I couldn't type fast enough to keep up with the theme. With our nation's freedom bridge hanging by a thread, would we allow it to crumble or turn around and rebuild? Within an hour, I sat back to read what I had written, and this poem was born.

Stand fast therefore in the liberty by which Christ has made us free, and do not be entangled again with a yoke of bondage.

—Galatians 5:1

Lasting Freedom?

It took the blood
Of many young men
To win the freedom
Of the Red, White, and Blue.

But

It only took the blood
Of one young man
To give us eternal freedom
Beyond the blue.

Where Has Time Gone?

It seems only yesterday some notable event occurred,
Shaking us to our roots or blessing us in a special way;
Sometime later, someone may ask, "Have you heard?"
Then thinking back, how has this affected my life today?

Whatever notable account stands out in our mind,
As we now take time to read these lines to the end,
This event may seem overwhelming at the time,
Or it could be a blessing designed by God's hand.

I trust that the focus of our work is much clearer,
As God's plan for our lives takes on a new rhyme;
Think back and ponder the events of the past year,
As we permit God to plant His goals in our mind.

As we allow the Holy Spirit to empower our lives,
For each one of us has a God-given job to do;
So let's not succumb to the world and its strife,
But love the lost souls to Christ by standing true.

Remember the truth in the Words of our Lord,
As we faithfully share His Love every day;
This Word is sharper than a two-edged sword,
So never hold back, but just give it away.

Someone may say it again, "Where has time gone?"
If our Lord has not returned or called us away;
Remember yesterday's gone, tomorrow may never come,
But we are promised God's blessing if we *do it today*.

Endorsements

"Elwood has a knack for putting words together to both rhyme and tell a story. On several occasions I have asked him to write a poem to celebrate a holiday or special event. He always comes through with just the right thing. It seems to just flow from him so easily. His poems can be either serious or silly. I'm sure you'll enjoy reading and gaining insight into his heart."

"... for his mouth speaks from what fills his heart." (NET Bible)

—Nancy Shank

"I can't claim to be a connoisseur of poetry, but even I find something special when I read a poem that resonates within me. Elwood has a passion for life and God. This passion clearly comes through in his poems. *The Poetry Bridge* covers a wide range of topics, from everyday moments to powerful life transforming events. Elwood's character and zest are reflected in his writings. Allow his humble nature and genuine love for God to speak to you and draw you closer to your Heavenly Father."

—Pastor Doug Bender

"When I first met Elwood and was introduced to his poetry, I was so impressed with his way of expressing life in a poetic way that I encouraged him to place these poems into book form so others can enjoy them as well. I did so because from the very first one I read, I sensed a love for the Lord and a love for life in a very real, yet practical way. I whole heartedly endorse this first book of Elwood's and trust he will consider writing a second for all to enjoy."

—Pastor Edward H. Eifert,
Newville Bible Church, Elizabethtown, PA.

"This is an inspiring and challenging collection of poems that will touch your heart in the many situations that life brings. It provides reassurance of God's love and his constant presence as well as praise to Him. As a willing vessel, Elwood offers poems given to him from the Lord. You will find his compilation a pleasure to read and to re-read, a gift from his heart to yours."

—Sandra Weinhold

CPSIA information can be obtained at www.ICGtesting.com
Printed in the USA
BVOW11s0322080714

358187BV00004B/17/P